Published in 2010 by New Holland Publishers (UK) Ltd
London ● Cape Town ● Sydney ● Auckland
www.newhollandpublishers.com

Garfield House, 86–88 Edgware Road, London W2 2EA, United Kingdom
80 McKenzie Street, Cape Town 8001, South Africa
Unit 1, 66 Gibbes Street, Chatswood, NSW 2067, Australia
218 Lake Road, Northcote, Auckland, New Zealand

10 9 8 7 6 5 4 3 2 1

A catalogue record for this book is available from the British Library.

ISBN 978 1 84773 807 3

Senior Editor: Kate Parker
Publisher: Aruna Vasudevan
Design and cover design: Vanessa Green, The Urban Ant Ltd

Reproduction by Pica Digital PTE Ltd, Singapore
Printed and bound in Malaysia by Tien Wah Press (PTE) Ltd

F**KING ANIMALS

Horny Rhinos and Humping Camels

NEW HOLLAND

Thank you

John-Rhys Dingle, Matt Irvine, Alistair King,
Helen Roper, Didz Parker, Sarah Powell,
Henry Russell, Grant Schreiber,
Rebekah Louise West, Sven Vrdoljak,
Professor T Yeboah VC and Greg Young

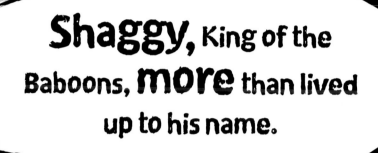

Shaggy, King of the Baboons, **more** than lived up to his name.

While at guide school Rover had **mastered** the unusual canine skill of the **two-legged reach-around.**

Just off the school bus and bearly legal

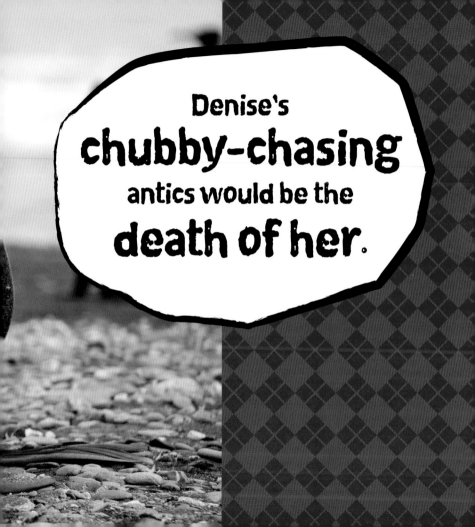

Always imagining that **kissing a frog** would turn the frog into a prince, Leia was **startled**, not to say **pissed off**, by this unexpected twist of fate.

He was as happy as a **pig in**, well, **another pig**.

It was **only** as the sun was going down, that it became clear why the locals called this **oddly-shaped** thorn bush **'Hard Dirty Rhino Sex'**.

Dan and Jen were **red-faced** with embarrassment when their **morning sport** was interrupted by a couple of humans **shagging** nearby.

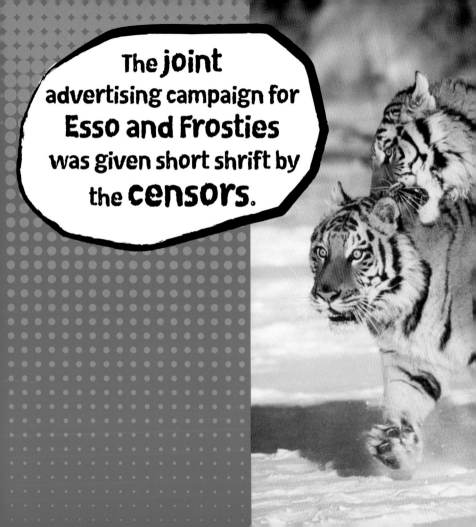

Quite a **load**
from
Mr Toad

With a heavy heart, Raymond **finally admitted** to himself that Vicky was probably more into the **tonne** of **cheap coke** she was busy hoovering up than she was him.

After **ten minutes** of trying, Kerry prayed he'd give up and take his oversized **red-hot stick of pain** away from her.

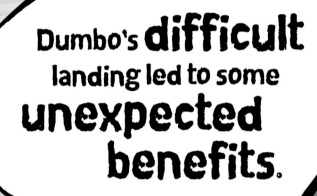

Mary-Lou shut her eyes and **thought** of the **money**. Frank was already 120 and it couldn't be **much longer** now...

Picture credits:

Thanks to the following copyright holders for allowing
their photographs to be used in this book:

Front cover: Yukihiro Fukuda/naturepl.com; page 6: Anup Shah/naturepl.com;
page 8: Getty Images/David Ward; page 10: Vivid Africa Photography/Alamy;
page 12: Kennan Ward/Corbis; page 14: Kevin Schafer/Corbis; page 16: George Sanker/naturepl.com;
page 18: Photolibrary.com; page 20: All Canada Photos/Alamy; page 22: Evan Bowen-Jones/Alamy;
page 24: DigitalVues/Alamy; page 26: Photoshot Holdings Ltd/Alamy; page 28: Tony Rolls/Alamy;
page 30: Barry Lewis/In Pictures/Corbis; page 32: Photolibrary.com;
page 34: Jim Zuckerman/CORBIS; page 36: Jeffry W. Myers/CORBIS;
page 38: Yukihiro Fukuda/naturepl.com; page 40: Getty Images/Gerald Fischer-Bernsteiner;
page 42: Tom Brakefield/CORBIS; page 44: Martin Harvey/CORBIS;
page 46: Photolibrary.com; page 48: Jane Burton/naturepl.com; page 50: Photolibrary.com;
page 52: Photolibrary.com; page 54: Suzi Eszterhas/naturepl.com;
page 56: Photolibrary.com; page 58: Photolibrary.com; page 60: Raymond Gehman/CORBIS;
page 62: Getty Images/Daniel J Cox; page 64: Getty Images/Alexander Nesbitt;
page 66: Photolibrary.com; page 68: Corbis Super RF / Alamy; page 70: Karl Ammann/naturepl.com;
page 72: Photolibrary.com; page 74: Photolibrary.com; page 76: Photolibrary.com;
page 78: Photolibrary.com; page 80: Getty Images/Nigel Dennis; page 82: Photolibrary.com;
page 84: Photolibrary.com; page 86: Frans Lanting/Corbis; page 88: Photolibrary.com;
page 90: Raed Qutena/epa/Corbis; page 92: Photolibrary.com;
page 94: Getty Images/Daniel J Cox